Finding Peace Power & Purpose

In 30 Days

〜∞〜

Shanekia Parker Rash

ISBN:978-0-578-64430-1

Dedication:

To my grandmother, who always remembered to save me a dance.
God gained an Angel, "My grandmother."

See you later:
Pearliemae Delcinue Williams

03-11-1929 to 06-29-2020

CONTENTS

Acknowledgement

I would like to acknowledge the help of all the people involved in the writing of this book and, more specifically, to God for giving me a vision. Without the support of my husband, parents, sisters, and motivators this book would not have become a reality.

My sincere gratitude goes to the valuable contributions of the reviewers, editors, and graphic designers. Sometimes what we fear the most causes us to walk through the fire to find our Peace, Power, and Purpose.

— **Shanekia Parker Rash**

Foreword

I can remember the day Shanekia was born. I was in the delivery room surrounded by several family members. The radio was playing R & B music. The OB staff had placed a mirror so I could watch myself deliver my first daughter. It was an experience I was not prepared for but was blessed to have had. This tiny beautiful baby girl was mine. All I could do was cry.

Growing up she always had to be in charge and have the last word. But life for her has always had its own set of challenges. Shanekia has always had a vision of what her life should look like. She has spent years trying to figure out herself, her purpose. She has struggled with depression, her marriage, her career, health, being a mother and her relationship with God.

We all have our share of problems in this world. Some may be more than others. The Children of Israel wandered in the desert for 40 years. Without a vision, we perish (Jeremiah 29:11). However, the Lord has a plan for all of us. We need to become engaged in what the Lord has for us to succeed. I was diagnosed with breast cancer in 2008. Through that experience God taught me that his grace is sufficient no matter what you are facing, and the miracles come after the trial of faith. If God is for us who can be against us (Romans 8:31)?

Foreword

It's important to understand that no one but God can fix everything we are going through, but the author has had to deal with a lot of highs and lows in her life. She has encountered many challenges, and most importantly, she has pushed forward, never giving in to her greatest fear, Failure.

Hopefully, in this book, you will discover experiences and gain a greater understanding of who you are and your purpose in life. You will begin to realize some of the fears in your life that have been holding you back and keeping you from succeeding in this life. Habakkuk 2:2 states, "Write the vision and make it plain." Write down your vision and forget what you DON'T HAVE. No shortcomings will stop God from providing. Be sincere, be firm, be true to yourself and open your heart to God. Believe in your vision.

— Tina Wright

Believe In Your Vision

Let's get right to it. The truth of the matter is you're feeling lost right now. There is an empty hole where fulfillment and joy used to sit. Now frustration and lack of confidence sit there. Each day you get up grudging more and more the fact that today is another day. A day that you regret, that you are not living in your peace, your power, and your purpose. You are choosing today to do the same routine that you have accepted to do each day. That is to get dressed slowly, to find the breakfast that suits you and to walk out of the door, and be enough, just enough.

Today, however, will be different. Today starts your journey. Your 30 days of purpose and fulfillment. Today is the day you become the new and improved you. You are more than just a number. You are the vision of success that you were born to be and are capable of being. With your head held high and your shoulders back. Release the number that you once were and embrace the vision that you are now becoming.

Welcome to your 30 days!

Sometimes one of the greatest uphill battles we face in life is that we are living so much for everyone else, that we forget to live for ourselves.

Each person you encounter has the same phrase to give you when you are asking for help with tasks. You're the carpool driver because they don't have time. The dry cleaner because they don't have time. The errand man because they don't have time. The cook and the maid because they don't have time. This leaves you not having time either.

No time for socialization. No time for entrepreneurship. No time for you! You feel as though life has defeated you once again. One of the greatest poets of all time said, "You will face many defeats in life, but never let yourself be defeated" (Maya Angelou). Think about all the challenges in life that you have been through, and you have faced in your life. Each of them you have defeated.

You have proven that you are a real fighter. You need to make sure you stay the course. Choose each battle wisely today because not everyone will be worth fighting. Make sure that every step you take and smile you make is done on Purpose.

"Spend today living in your Purpose and make sure you keep track of your results."
Shanekia Parker Rash

What do you feel like your Purpose is in life?

_____

_____

_____

_____

_____

_____

_____

_____

_____

_____

_____

_____

_____

_____

_____

_____

_____

Did you encounter any trials or battles today that you had to walk away from?

_____

_____

_____

_____

_____

_____

_____

_____

_____

_____

_____

_____

_____

_____

_____

_____

How much stronger are you because you chose not to let yourself be defeated?

_____
_____
_____
_____
_____
_____
_____
_____
_____
_____
_____
_____
_____
_____
_____
_____
_____
_____

"If you cannot do great things, do small things in a great way."
— *Napoleon Hill*

Did you know that it is the small and simple things that we simply choose NOT to do each day that keep us from reaching our goals? It is not that you cannot achieve them. It is that you are not in the mind frame to do so.

So how do you go about fixing your mindset? Start by adjusting what you can see. You are holding on to things that you cannot control, and while it may not seem to be an issue, in reality, this is blocking your growth. Use today to focus on the things that you can control that are keeping you from being the best you. Let go of the bed. No one ever accomplished anything by sleeping. Forgive those who have angered you. Holding on to this resentment is keeping you from moving forward to greatness. Forget the job interview that did not go well days, weeks, or even months ago, because it was not for you. These all seem to be small things, but they are all hurting YOU in a big way.

These are all small tasks that need to be accomplished, be great at getting them done.

CHOOSING *Yourself*

Day 3

When is the last time you read a good book? I mean really sat down and dug deep into the pages. Sat intrigued by what the author had to say because you had time. Do you even remember the title of the last book you read (and books for your higher educational degree do not count)? Can you remember what the author of the long-awaited nicely written page-turning novel said? Probably not, but that's ok because today is a day to change that.

Did you know that sometimes the answer is NO? It's not maybe later, not today, or perhaps some other day. It's NO! Today is the day you reclaim the usage of the word no. The two-letter word that we often forget to use when we are not living for ourselves but living to be a vessel for someone else to use and abuse. Not NO in an obscene and insecure way, but no in such a way that you reclaim at least 30 minutes of your well-deserved time back today.

Figure out what aspects in your life you're only doing to please others, and simply say NO. Work on reclaiming at least 30 mins of your week back today. Are you not worth 30 mins?

Learning to Choose Yourself

Imagine a typical week in your life. Take a moment to think about all of your obligations and the things you do for other people. These obligations include family and work, as well. Take a minute to list those things next to the image below. Start from the bottom to the top.

10. _____

9. _____

8. _____

7. _____

6. _____

5. _____

4. _____

3. _____

2. _____

1. _____

Take a moment to look at your list. Are you running "hot"? Do you find yourself having more time for others than yourself? Are you happy?

What are three things you can say no to this week?

1. _____

2. _____

3. _____

Day 4

Ever been in the middle of a project and just wanted to give in? You're not sure if this is even what you want in life or if you're headed in the right direction. Flashbacks and visions in your mind show you being successful in your past life. Did you graduate top of your class, honor roll student, participated in clubs or groups? Now that life has shown up and taken control, where are you? You feel like you are in the middle of nowhere drowning, and no one can see you.

I see you.

I see your visions, your Purpose, your dreams, and your goals.

It is not a matter of how you are going about doing things on a daily basis. It is a matter of the why.

You have just forgotten your why.

> *"Wisdom is in the principal thing; therefore, get wisdom. And in all thy getting get understanding."*
> — *Proverbs 4:7*

You can't take it with you. What you're seeking I mean. Often, we spend our lives seeking materials things such as money, cars, and fame. However, if all of them were stripped away from you, what would you have left?

Some of the most important things that we have and can see daily we take for granted. We are in search of immaterial happiness. Consider this, if you had to build your legacy again brick by brick, stone by stone, could you do it? Do you have the wisdom, the knowledge, and the power to recreate what you have done? If not begin to gain wisdom so that whatever is taken from you, you can rebuild it.

Start gaining wisdom so that you can gain assets.

Think about your life. What things build up your legacy? What things are you building on?

Look at the bricks above. Make a list below that describes your legacy and make sure to include things you have learned and skills you have developed.

1. _____

2. _____

3. _____

4. _____

5. _____

6. _____

7. _____

8. _____

9. _____

10. _____

11. _____

12. _____

The most amazing dream once occurred in my head. I dreamed that the world was a place of equality. That men and women were on the same scale. I dreamed the word freedom was only used to describe the release of school children from a long day of school. My friends and family supported my visions. My goals were that much more achievable because I had a team of people to push, no PROPEL me forward.

Then I woke up. Once I woke up from this vivid and refined dream, I realized that I was alone and that my dreams were just that. Dreams. I was not free, and because of this, my visions, goals, and wants were not supported by others. My friends, my family, and my supporters instantly told me of their disdained disapproval and how much they thought their ideas for my future suited me better. Sound familiar?

Your dream killers were not meant to be sharers of your vision. Not everyone will believe in your dreams. That's because God didn't entrust the vision to them. Remember that the race is for you. Trust in the vision that you have, and you cannot go wrong.

One of the most precious possessions we have in life is time. Time waits for no one. It reverts for no one, and it keeps no records of wrong. Time is unforgiving and doesn't like to be wasted. Time is not a rewarder of those who misuse or abuse it.

I often have a hard time focusing on things that really matter. I allow others to abuse my time, and in turn, it may, NO, it will cost me. Time is the one thing in life that no one will respect if you don't require them to. Use today to focus on having a deep admiration for your time. Value your time. Put a price on your time and make it stand. Regardless of whether your charging a fee, make sure others know you value you.

Placing value on your time increases **NET** worth **INTERNALLY**.

TIME...
IS...
RICELESS

Do you value your time? Make a list of things that you find yourself doing for others for **free** that you could be paid for.

Now develop an exit strategy. Practice saying "no" today.

"Learning how to say no is learning how to balance your life."
— Alli Doubek

Day 8

I remember like it was yesterday. I stood at the door, proud of the outfit I picked out. I was even excited because I had styled my own hair. I left the house with my head held high, proud of the decisions that I had made. From 8 am until 3:50 pm, I was satisfied and OK with what I had done and my accomplishments. Immediately after school, I was met by my sister. She said something that changed my outlook on the 8 to 3:50 me. She said, "You should take more pride in the way you look; as you grow older, people will judge you based upon your appearance."

Genesis 11:1-9 tells us the story of the tower of Babel. This is a narrative that tells us why languages are "confused" or why there are so many different languages. I believe it was at that moment I realized that she and I, well we spoke two different languages. Always remember that God not only uses your wins, but he also uses your mistakes and your battles as necessary building blocks to your tower.

Take each building block. The block of mistake, battles, haters, wins, disappointment, and necessary trials and use them to create your tower of greatness. I love that God uses every one of our mistakes and turns them for our good. No matter what they think you should be doing, God knows. Moving forward towards your goals is necessary.

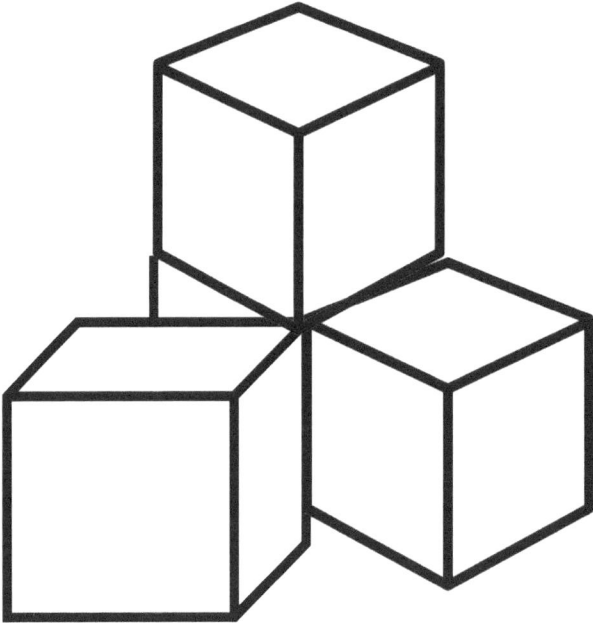

> *"So God created man in his own image, in the image of God created he him; male and female created he them."*
> — *Genesis 1:27*

What's wrong with you? It's hard to figure out why you keep slipping in and out of this slippery slope of depression. You have moments in your life where you are on a high, and no one can get you down. Then there are those moments in your life where you are so low; it's hard to get up, get dressed, and make it out of the door. I completely understand what it means to feel defeated by the struggles of life and the pain of life, but you cannot continue to let life get the best of you.

How is your relationship with God? In Genesis 1:27, we find that we are created in his image. Are you willing to have your relationship with him examined? Take a moment and write down your feelings about your genuine relationship with God.

How is your relationship with yourself? To have a deeper relationship with God is to have a deeper relationship with yourself. We were created in his image. I challenge you to use today and this day forward to not only work on your relationship with God but to work on how you see yourself.

Describe your relationship with God

_____

_____

_____

_____

_____

_____

_____

_____

_____

_____

_____

_____

_____

_____

_____

_____

_____

_____

Describe your relationship with yourself

Our relationship with ourselves is the most important one we will ever have. How you see yourself is how everyone else will as well. Write positive things about yourself in the mirror below and read them aloud.

Day 10

Your wait is officially over. I know, you, like me have been waiting on a sign. Waiting on God to come down from Heaven. To pick you up, wrap you up in his loving arms, squeeze you tight and say TODAY IS THE DAY. Guess what? You don't need a sign to pursue your dreams, you just need to do it.

There are two types of dreamers in the world; those who dream in color and those who dream in black and white. Those who dream in color tend to have vivid dreams that have sequels. These dreams can last for months and usually end up coming to fruition. Those who dream in black and white take the safe route. They dream of cautionary tales or climbing the corporate ladder and of only taking the calculated risk.

The difference between the two types of dreamers is that those who dream in color dared to pursue them. Chose to be the Steve Jobs, the Tyler Perry, and the Shanekia Parker Rash of your times.

Do you dream in color or in black and white?

Do you dream in color or black and white?

———————————————————————————
———————————————————————————
———————————————————————————
———————————————————————————
———————————————————————————
———————————————————————————
———————————————————————————
———————————————————————————
———————————————————————————
———————————————————————————
———————————————————————————
———————————————————————————
———————————————————————————
———————————————————————————
———————————————————————————
———————————————————————————
———————————————————————————

Day 11

Name your price: When I first started as a Real Estate agent in 2010-2011, I was eager to be the top-selling agent in my firm. I did what I thought was necessary to be in the business. I began to educate myself. However, education was not enough. I began to walk the streets. I knocked on doors and cold-called. All of this while pregnant with my 2nd child. My talents and my skills were not enough. I needed a sell.

Cutting my commission, buying a home warranty, or cleaning a house anything to make a deal work was my go-to. That still just was not enough. It was knowledge.

Ben Franklin said, "An investment in knowledge always pays the best interest." It turns out, it not only pays the best interest, but it also yields the best return in results. Seeking out mentors, gaining knowledge in my career field, and investing in things that help set me apart is what turned the pages for me. What investment should you make in life or your career that will yield the best return for you?

One of the most rewarding things about being a wife and a mother are the intimate private moments we get to have alone with each family member. As a mother, I have a bond with each one of my children. I have had the privilege of carrying them, nursing them, and taking care of them while they are sick. As a wife, I have the honor of building my husband up, supporting him in his endeavors, celebrating his accomplishments, and being there as a help meet in life. With all of these, I believe my most prized duty is being their secret keeper.

Whose secret keeper are you and who is your secret keeper?

Lots of people entrust you with their secrets and expect you not to tell. They choose you as their burden bearer. You entrust your secrets to others and swear them to secrecy. Remember that broken people cannot help you put your broken pieces back together. Like any puzzle, every piece has another piece that fits just right. Some secrets are only meant to be shared with God, the real burden bearer. I have found that writing my thoughts and true meditation with God are the best ways to empty my mind. Know who to entrust your secrets to, as not everyone is worthy of being your secret keeper.

The crowd is silent, patiently awaiting the next move. Number 15 moves down the field, spins and steals the ball. He passes the ball to number 21. They both move forward at a steady pace juggling the ball toward the goal. The competitors approach looking to stop the ball from penetrating the goal. The kick is too strong. The crowd goes wild! Ladies and gentlemen, the corner kick from number 15 was intense; it was fast, it was furious, it was, it was, it was. It was the only highlight in the 1-hour and 20-minute game.

My son is a soccer player, but not just any soccer player. He is good for his age (he is 10). At this age, we don't get to see much action in a game, so we live for the moments. After every game he says, "Mom or Dad, did you see my….…." And then he will give us his one highlight or favorite part of the game that he feels like was amazing. We reply, "it was okay, but son, you can't have just one highlight in the entire game." Is this true? We could allow him to be satisfied with just being good, but each game we see more and more improvement in his performance.

We see his willingness and his desire to be a stronger, faster, and better player. He desires to practice more. He wants to learn more about the game and learn more about the players of the game. He even wishes to accept criticism and work on perfecting the things that he has done wrong.

What is your one highlight in life?

You can continue to allow your-self to be average. An average carpenter, DJ, mother, father, radio host, nurse, and so forth. You can also choose to take control of YOU and desire to be stronger, faster, and better at whom you want to be and what you are choosing to do every single day. Choose to turn your one highlight into a lifetime of achievements.

Tradition tells us that the oldest child is the responsible one. The routine of taking care of the other children, making sure the house is kept, and that things are in order tend to fall on firstborn children. Life, however, hands down different rules. Like the cornerstone to any building, the child who shows the most potential will be the one who is set as a reference point or leader. The responsible child is used in determining the entire formula of the whole family. This could be the middle child or even the youngest, depending on how close they are in age. This responsible child becomes the cornerstone of the family, the pillar, and the one who everyone leans on to make sure things go well no matter what the storm is.

Are you the family rock? If a meeting of the minds needs to be called, are you responsible for calling it? If a family member is in trouble, are you responsible for finding a solution to the issue?

Who is your cornerstone? Often, being the cornerstone or pillar for everyone else leaves you feeling lost. You don't feel like there is anyone there for you to help you when you are in need. You are always encouraged to be the strong one because you're needed.

You are encouraged to be the levelheaded one because it is expected. When do you get to be you?

In Exodus 14:14, it reads, "The Lord shall fight for you, and ye shall hold your peace." The Lord will fight for you, just like he did for Moses. Know that not every battle that your family, friends, and acquaintances have is meant for you to join in. Some things need to be left for the Lord. You can sit out of a few fights.

You're allowed to cry, to be angry, rejoice, to be happy, to be in love, to have accomplishments, and to miss family dinners. Give yourself room to grieve over the loss of past relationships and to feel pain. You have spent so much time being strong for everyone else today is the day you can be strong for you.

Use today to be your own rock. Give yourself the ability to breathe and grow into and know the new you that you are trying to develop. Write down how you feel about becoming a cornerstone for yourself. Write the things you are willing to change to be strong for you. If you don't start now, your building will fall apart, simply because you're too busy holding everyone else's up.

How can you become your own cornerstone?

Day 15

Recently a popular magazine company put out an amazing cover shoot. This cover displayed a beautiful African model with retro vibes. Melanin was on 1000. A cleaver high waisted ensemble was used with bright colors. Red, yellow, and a pale blue to be exact. She was draped in a sheer gown that dragged the floor. Her accessories highlighted her outfit and she sported an Afro that would make anyone take notice.

As I looked at the glow that was coming from her and read the nicely written piece, my focus kept going to the watermark that was softly placed in the bottom right-hand corner of the page. I had accidentally stumbled upon the stylist, and that is honestly all I had really wanted.

Now, the sister was gorgeous, but let's be honest, whoever designed this outfit was the real showstopper. Upon further research and stalking of her Instagram, Facebook, and his. I was able to discover his website and view many of his pieces.

How are you leaving your mark on the world? It's ok to follow the rules of Matthew 6:33. I understand that we want the benefits of our father in heaven to reward us.

I also know that it's okay to receive credit for being great and doing great things. If you refuse to leave your mark on the world, how will anyone know how great you truly are?

Leave your mark now, so we will remember how great you were later.

High School was an interesting time for me. Debate team, band, cheer squad, drama club, stars (volunteer program to mentor kids), and the track team. There was no time to be mediocre. My parents didn't have money to pay for college, and I was determined to make sure I received a scholarship. Track was never my go-to sport, but it was one that I knew college recruiters really paid attention to, so it was on the list. My races consisted of the 4 X 400-meter relay and the hurdles.

One meet, one of our racers did not show up. I watched as our coach paced frantically back and forth across the track. The team and I jokingly mocked him and made jokes under our breath, because our own race was already complete. I could see the worry in his face as the announcer called the race again.

"All runners for the 1600 report to the line." Coach paced again (any harder he would have burned a hole in the grass). Finally, he stopped. He looked up and frantically yelled "Parker (my maiden name) hit the line." "Hit the line? Hit the line?" I reluctantly, with my head held high, went over and hit the line. Now, you may be wondering why I didn't ask questions, Me too, but I'm glad I didn't because I placed 2nd.

You are riding the bench right now because you're afraid to hit the line. You are scared to take losses, you're afraid of not being able to make it without a plan B, or you're just straddling the fence. Imagine how much further in life, you would be if you would just stop asking questions and hit the line. Today is a hit the line type of day, are you up for the challenge?

What's stopping you from hitting the line?

⟋⟍⟋⟍

_____

_____

_____

_____

_____

_____

_____

_____

_____

_____

_____

_____

_____

_____

Day 17

"Pray without ceasing."
— Thessalonians 5:17

From my earliest memory as a child, I can remember two things: firm discipline and a praying mother. If we listen to music, whether It be Gospel, R&B, Hip Hop, or Country, none of the artist are afraid to say that their mother, grandmother, wife, etc. prayed for them. Do you love yourself enough to pray for your needs?

Refer to Matthew 7:7 and Matthew 21:22. Establish your gateway to heaven. Pray without ceasing. God loves to hear from his children. He knows your needs and is waiting to supply.

Maya Angelou was known for leaving you breathless with her words. Leaving you captivated and speechless hanging on by a thread wanting more. Tupac was a lyrical genius. When he touched the mic and hit the booth, he spoke the truth. Their work lives on because we continue to circulate their greatness. We pass it down from generation to generation, making sure that the integrity is intact and that the impact of the art is there.

We all can be significant and leave an impact in some way. We may not be a poet or lyrical genius, but each of us has a gift that will make room for us. Don't allow your gift to be influenced by others, and don't hide your gifts or talents because you're afraid someone else possesses more.

In Matthew Chapter 25, we find the parable of talents. The one that impresses me the most is the servant with the one. He has the most potential to become the greatest. you too, can increase your talent. Even your one gift or talent will make room for you.

> *"Everybody's at war with different things. I'm at war with my own heart sometimes."*
> — *Tupac Shakur*

Psychologically we assume we can separate the good in our lives from the bad. We can help our children, our friends, our coworkers, and neighbors to eliminate their problems. We help solve and rewrite their stories, but we cannot revise our own. Their stories were so much easier because of our position. Being able to be the judge and jury in another person's trial is natural. To become the judge and jury in your life is more complicated.

A cycle is defined as a series of events that are regularly repeated in the same order. Johnathan McReynolds said it best in his song Cycles. He asks, "Didn't I conquer this last year? Tell me what I missed 'cause I fear that it's coming back up again."

What bad habits are you allowing to come back in your life continually? Are you dealing with a relationship that is unhealthy, and you're struggling with letting go? Waiting on them to treat you right, give you more, and for the feeling of emptiness to leave you... you can and will waste your entire life waiting on a person to change.

If you feel empty while you are in a relationship with someone, then there is no need for you to make room for them in your life. You are giving them priority status when you are just an option to them.

Use today to break out of the cycles you are in. What cycle did you think you conquered but fell back into? Let's conquer it together.

In 2006 I left everything that was comfortable to me to join the Air Force. I was running from all of the trials that I had back home. Picking up and leaving would allow me to forget everything and everyone that had ever hurt, looked me over or betrayed me. I told no one I was enlisting, not even my mom. She dropped me off at the hotel, and the next day I was on my way to be an Airman.

I was sworn in and boarded the plane. I have no idea what happened in between. I just knew I wanted to wipe away my past, my mistakes, my trials, and begin this new journey. Nothing was going to stop me from becoming the new and improved me.

Once we had reached our destination, I quickly exited the plane and gathered my bags. I, like everyone else, had packed everything I owned. I was not coming back. My fancy bag had rollers on the bottom. I dragged it down the terminal runway, confidently. You could hear the click-clack, click-clack, click-clack. I was headed to the new me, and no one was going to block my victory. I was determined Not to look back.

I looked up with the biggest grin on my face. There stood in front of me; the biggest white man I had ever seen, in a funny looking green suit with a hat. His face was as rosy as Santa's cheeks on Christmas day. He was not as happy to see me as I was to see him. He placed his nose firmly on mine and said, "listen up, you brought this baggage you carry it."

You can try to run from the problems in your life. You can even pack up and leave the state, but eventually, you will have to meet them where they are. An unanswered problem or issue is like dragging your baggage through the terminal, thinking that the things you left behind, are not still piling up.

Do not allow things such as being angry with someone control your emotions. Apologize and move on. Do not let failure dictate your life, retake the test, and move on. It is never too late to be who or what God has called you to be. The only thing that is stopping you is you.

What are you running from that you need to face? A test you cannot pass CDL, LSAT, MCAT? A relationship that you need to let go of?

Let's figure it out.

I've always wanted to be average, but that's not in the cards for me. My choice of careers, cars, and even clothing has always been unique to me. Am I complaining about being different? No, but must I stand out so much?

The debate has always been that I've wanted to be a stay at home mom. I have always wanted to stay home and watch my little ones grow and be the support system for my husband while he takes on the world. I've wanted to watch him run circles in the political arena. Allow him to be the force that drives crowds and keep people captivated. I have always wanted to be his biggest fan.

Over the last few years of our marriage, I have spent time molding and shaping our future for him to take over the world! I express an idea and expect him to take it over and RUN! Unfortunately, he is not as motivated as I would hope. My plan for him ends up being an idea I end up running and pushing off on him. It becomes successful, but not without the push from me.

So, I lay there thinking… is he not mold-able? He doesn't want it bad enough. I research and try to find ways to convince him to take on my ideas of success and push him forward. He rejects my advances, again and again, God finally tells me, "Shanekia, these moments are not for him; they are for you."

God uses the oddest moments in our lives to mold us. A death, a birth, a 2 AM wake up call. Whatever your moment is, make sure you're paying attention. We want so hard to see success manifest in our lives. We are daring to get it by any means necessary. We push our kids on the field to hard. We make our spouses work eight jobs to get the bills paid and help us field our entrepreneurship. We even work holidays and overtime on our hourly job, so that we can say we are climbing the corporate ladder.

At the end of the journey, are you genuinely molding yourself into the person you want to be and someone you can truly be proud of? Are you someone who can stand at the gates of Heaven and receive a well done? Or are you just pushing buttons to see how quickly the elevator can get to the top?

The art of there is always tomorrow. Think about this exact day seven months ago. What if you did; what if you had… when you wanted to go? If you had taken the job, then where would you be now? If you had mailed off the application, would you be sitting in the front row of the class? Whom were you waiting for? What were you waiting for? Whom were you expecting to do it for you?

Victor Kiam said, "Procrastination is opportunity's assassin."

Are you allowing the lack of your ability to be self-driven to kill your movement in life? The issue with being a procrastinator is that YOU are forgetting that each opportunity has an expiration date. There is this general unwritten assumption that whatever task that needs to be done will be waiting for you when you feel compelled to complete it.

The lie detector test has determined; that is a lie.

Wives who need affection will seek it from someone else. Children will act out. Supervisors who need a job completed will replace you with a more efficient employee or machine. A task that needs to be done will be handed down to people who are more skillful than you to complete them.

Do not allow procrastination to kill your movement in life. You will become an artist staring at a blank canvas with no brush or paint or a chef standing in a kitchen with no ingredients. You cannot perform.

Procrastination can cause an unhealthy shift in our lives. By neglecting and putting off responsibilities and goals, your life will have less balance. List everything that you could have done and should have done that you have procrastinated and think of what things you can

1. _____

2. _____

3. _____

4. _____

5. _____

6. _____

"You can, you should, and if you're brave enough to start, you will."
— *Stephen King*

Real Estate has been this thing that I have been doing for a while now. The benefit of it is that I get to meet some beautiful people who give amazing advice. The downside of Real Estate is that I get to meet some beautiful people who give bad advice. My absolute favorite part about being an agent is the closets. Each closet is different and has its own story. The one similarity that each closet has is the shelves.

Not every single person I speak to in my life has positivity bursting out of their ears. The ones who do really scare me. I know that when they get mad, their head probably does a full 360. Smoke comes out of their ears. Their eyes turn red, and they rub their foot back and forth on the ground like a raging bull getting ready to charge.

Scary sight, I know. Those who are realistic and speak positivity I like to keep around. These types of people keep me grounded. It was never meant for you to take everything someone tells you and use it at face value. Somethings must be put on the closet shelf and kept for later.

Now, negative comments; meaning those things that ruin the way you look at yourself. Place them on the shelf and leave them in the house for the movers to chunk out when you leave or discard them right away. Every day may not be useful, but you can find positivity in every day.

What do you want to be remembered for? Start training yourself to be the keeper of positivity.

Be the keeper of joy, and don't allow people to take it from you. Use things that can help you stay the course. Began to use affirmations change your daily habits and change the people you surround yourself with. Let go of the things that bring negative energy into your life. Start small and you will see significant results.

> *"You can, you should, and if you're brave enough to start, you will."*
> — *Stephen King*

There is not one adult who does not spend his or her life searching.

Some spend countless years navigating from job to job. Some are free-spirited and never get a job; they "live off of what the land provides." Whatever you decide or search after, someone has found some way to ruin your way of getting to your Purpose. People challenge the way you move towards your goals, dreams, success, or Purpose because they cannot see the end results. Instead of enjoying the journey, you find yourself dreading the one thing that is supposed to bring you joy—finding yourself. You tried college and it just wasn't what you thought it would be. The corporate ladder was not the climb you felt it should have been. So you are more of a free-spirited soul, and that's ok! What do you do when others do not see what you want them to?

Is this the real issue? Often, we are so caught up in not knowing where to be in life that; we just throw ourselves into ANYTHING thinking others cannot see the true beauty in the free ME. Is it that they can't see the beauty in the free you, or that they can see the downward spiral in the depressed you? It's ok not to know who you are to be lost and to be still searching even now at this point in your life. Speak positive things to yourself.

Create positive habits and begin to change. I believe in affirmations! They truly help speak life to every situation you may encounter. Use today not only to craft your affirmation but to make a commitment to yourself to recite it each day.

"May your actions of today affirm your success for tomorrow."
— Shanekia Parker Rash

Affirmations

How to Write Affirmations:

Step 1: Make sure your affirmations start with I or My because you are affirming your ability to achieve or excel at something.

Step 2: Always write your affirmations in the present tense and make them short and easy to remember.

Step 3: Turn your negatives into positives.

Example: I cannot achieve the success I want.

Affirmation: I can achieve success.

Craft your own affirmation in the space below. Say it aloud to yourself throughout the day.

Day 25

"Leave only the stains that will stand the test of time."
— *Shanekia Parker Rash*

I woke up that morning not as hurried as usual. 5:00 a.m. stared at me and I knew it was my time to commune with God. I wanted to look for excuses, but none came my way. I arose and began to pray, meditate, and read. My house was quiet and the rain hitting the rooftop made it more mellow than I could ever have hoped for. After an hour, I retired back to bed and drifted back off to sleep. At 6:15, the alarm rang, and my husband jumped up to go and wake the kids. He reminded me that we needed to hurry, or they would be late. I explained it's cold and rainy let them sleep in — the perfect excuse to allow me to sleep later.

My children woke around 8:30 and were ready for breakfast, but I wasn't prepared to move. Keldrick (my husband) had left for his doctors' appointment. At this moment, it was decision time. I had to decide to be a parent or go back to sleep. As I turned over to let my face hit the cold side of the pillow, I realized this isn't what good mothers do. After a few hours, I finally forced myself to get up. I put on my good jeans, my Converse sneakers, and my red lipstick (for the power of course). Not just any red lipstick. The kind that lasts all day, but leaves a mark wherever you go, so you're not forgotten. Now, I had nowhere important to go, but it was the moment that I realized I couldn't let me defeat me. Even though I had no real place to go, I made sure I left my mark everywhere.

I kissed my two-year-old. Boy did that leave the house on edge. Everyone thought she ran into a wall and injured herself, but nope it was just Mommy's stained IM-perfection. I kissed Daddy's bald head and Cameryn my 10-year old's too. The mark I believe that I left will stand the test of time, however, is the picture I gave to my 8year-old daughter. It was a memory from my little treasure box that will last her a lifetime.

What stains are you leaving behind that will last? What do you want to be remembered for?

We all have imperfections that leave stains, but that doesn't make us bad.

"Polish your imperfections, so that your stains make a lasting impression."
— Shanekia Parker Rash

The new car smell traps 1 in 5 families every hour (lol by my stats). Stepping onto the lot, we had our head in the game. We were a united front. Nothing and no one was going to keep us from our goal. Those goals consisted of pricing the vehicles to compare competitors and NOT to leave the lot with a new car. My husband and I have this down to a science. The best time for us to go is during the summer.

Why do you ask? Summer is the time I can walk the lot. I browse the vehicles, check their safety ratings, prices, and the essential things before sitting in the seat and smelling the new car. During the fall and winter, its cold. My number one goal is to find a car and see if the heat works! Who cares about the rest? Failure always hits us during the Fall and Winter on the car lot. I get trapped by the smell.

Recently we purchased a new vehicle. This was not by choice. We grudgingly walked the lot looking at cars trying to find the one with the best gas mileage and the lowest price. After a few test drives, we left with what I deemed to be the perfect fit for our family.

10 mins after we left the lot, I approached a stop sign, and the traffic was unusually high— the car cutoff. I panicked. My husband and I looked at each other, and we immediately said, this one must be defective.

During our test drive of this vehicle, it did the same thing. We attributed it to the low gas (the gas light was on). We turned around, called our dealer, and headed back to the car lot to exchange our brand-new car with the issues. Our salesman came out, pushed a button, and said, "oh, this is the gas-saving feature for this car. To not use it during a drive press here." What did we do wrong? We looked at the safety ratings, we checked out the gas mileage, we test drove the car, but we did not ever open the owner's manual. Weeks later, I learned; my car had no CD player nor any special features about the gas. You guessed it. I still haven't read the manual.

So many things in life come so naturally to you. You're able to cook dinner without reading the recipe. Pass a class without studying and the list goes on. It seems like the things that matter most to you are the things that you see as the most difficult to understand. Life seems to be dishing out blows that you don't have the manual for.

Matthew 21:22 tells us that, "And all things, whatsoever ye shall ask in prayer, believing ye shall receive." I am a firm believer that the Bible is the greatest manual ever written, and if you just open it, read it and be sincere in your desire, it shall be given. Things that you want to be manifested in the real world must be placed in your spirit, written down and made plain. Habakkuk 2:2 tells us to write the vision and make it plain.

Write down your vision, "forget what you DON'T HAVE, no lack will stop God from providing. Be sincere, be firm, be true to yourself, and open your heart to God."
— Shanekia Parker Rash

Vision

Now it is your turn to create your vision. Create your vision below of who you see yourself becoming and what you want to accomplish.

_____

_____

_____

_____

_____

_____

_____

_____

_____

_____

_____

_____

_____

_____

_____

_____

Vision

Use this page to write the key points you see for yourself and your life. Look back at this frequently to remind yourself what you are working towards.

> "Communication is the one thing that can break the cycle of distrust in family, friendship, and familiarity. When we choose to be honest at all costs the right people will stick around."
> — Shanekia Parker Rash

My mom is the best gift giver of all times. She always gives the gifts that drive my husband and me crazy. We can remember the pony that was bigger than our living room couch. My daughter was terrified of it. The race car that she bought my son (one that he could drive). The air hockey table (that we had no room for), the pressure cooker, instant pot, and my husband's all-time favorite the Christmas cookies! The gift, however, that keeps on giving is the Betta fish she bought Kyleigh. For our 2-year-old, this fish was love at first sight. She wanted to hold the fish, kiss the fish, and like many toddlers, she wanted her own fish. Being the good parents, we are we decided to go to the pet store and buy another fish. We could just add it to the tank that my mom bought with the Betta fish, right?

NEWS FLASH! My mom is not the best gift-giver of all times for no reason. She will FOREVER hold this title. My mom bought the one fish that must be in the tank by himself. The Betta fish, also known as the Siamese fighting fish, are highly territorial. They are prone to high levels of aggression and will attack other fish if housed in the same tank. During our trip, we not only learned about the Betta.

We learned we needed a new tank, food, and all the other items for the new fish. We now have 2 tanks and 3 fish. The most important thing is we have 2 happy little girls. Each day the girls rush to feed their fish. They both head to their tanks and watch them swim. They drop the food in and laugh as the fish rush to eat.

I dropped the two school-aged little ones off first. They yelled, "We love you!" and kissed their little sister. I pulled up at the sitter's house and placed my car in the park. As I leaned back to ask Catie if she was ready to go, she replied, "Mom, my bish no working." "What do you mean," I asked? She repeated it. "My bish no working. It's probably dead. "Catie honey, who told you the fish was dead?" "Nobody, it's no working. I'm ready to go, momma."

I was in complete shock that she knew the fish was dead, and that she could communicate that to me in her own way. What was my next move? Truth is, I did not have one. We thought that by not telling her, we were protecting her. In life, we keep secrets from our loved ones, secrets that sometimes hurt us to keep. We think it is protecting them. It's not. There is no hurt like being hurt by someone you love.

As a parent, we are sometimes overprotective. As children, we are used by our parents. We are working hard to gain their love or feeling guilty because we want to pay them back for the years of raising that they gave us. That is impossible. You have taken time, to be honest with yourself within these 30 days of peace, power, and purpose. Now it's time to communicate that same level of honesty to those around you. Why did you choose to take over the family business? Why are you choosing to live at home? Why do you constantly take on the assignments at work, but allow others to take the credit?

You're the architect that designed the home and interior designer that placed the furniture in all the right places, but the credit went to the developer who didn't lay one single brick or tile. Why?

Day 28

I am THE best marketing and branding strategist that you will find. Clients bring me their ideas. We have strategy sessions about their business, their goals, and what they want to achieve. Through hard work and skill, it happens. I remember working with a YouTuber and motivational speaker. The most amazing part about working with her was that she didn't know that she was a YouTuber and motivational speaker.

This young lady enrolled in a course I ran called Brand It Like A Boss. Through one on one's, selective group sessions and claims to fame. my lady graduated from the course with flying colors. She didn't know what she was in the class for (she had no direction or selected path). She just knew she wanted to be successful, and she wanted to know my secrets.

Receipts (reviews) fell, and I was elated. Not only did she graduate from the course, but she started getting paid from her channel. She started traveling, speaking, and getting paid. This little one didn't need my secrets. She needed the tools. More importantly, she needed to have the willingness to put in the work.

I recently read a post (on Facebook) where a young lady lost 97lbs on her weight loss journey. Her post was flooded by comments of people who wanted to know how she lost the weight. Does this matter? If you are not disciplined or willing to put in the work, knowing the secrets, the trials, or the tools won't help you.

> *"I'm BOLD enough to give you my entire bag of tricks, are you disciplined enough to apply them?"*
> *— Shanekia Parker Rash*

It was bedtime for my two-year-old. We had just finished bath time and eating dinner. Now the real challenge was putting her down to bed. Ignoring the responsibility of doing this had become a sport for my husband and I. We can literally roll dice or pull cards to see who has to chase her down to get her in the bed. I sat in the bed and cracked open my newest book by Common, "Let love have The last word."

My husband sat at the end of the bed and began to search through his phone at the latest foolery on Facebook, I assume. I tried to ignore the noise that rang from the mouth of my overly excited two-year-old. I was failing. She pointed frantically to letters she recognized on the pages and loudly yelled! Mommy C – L – D look. It's an L- A- and D.

I stopped and began to acknowledge her, and in doing so I realized she was right. There was more there than what I was able to see. Sometimes we are so focused on just getting the job done that we don't realize we are missing pieces to our puzzle. You are rushing to begin the story and before you know it, you are sitting at the end and you can't remember what the story was about.

Are you rushing to skip to the end of your story, work or trial, because you don't like the setup? Psalms 139:16 tells us that God knew us before we were here. Just like a chapter in any well-written novel. If we skip to the end or tear out pages, we will miss the much-needed lesson or the entire meaning of the story. LIVE your full story. The pain, the ups, the downs, and TELL it all. Your truth can heal someone.

Day 30

This is not your first self-help book. Let's make it your last. In 2003 I graduated from high school and went straight to college. I had dreams, ambitions, and goals. When classes started, I had frat parties, house parties, and lots of tardies (I was always late to class). Even though I thought about everything I wanted to do, I never wrote it down. I stepped on that college campus with no plan. Dr. Myles Monroe said, "Develop a plan so strong that time will submit to it and change will become its servant."

Don't allow this to be just another self-help book. Make it THE self-help book that changed the course of your life. Sometimes we have to reach back, to truly go forward.

Define your goals more clearly. Plan the change that you want to see in yourself this time. If you do, it will last a lifetime.
— Shanekia Parker Rash

When setting goals for yourself it is important to set SMART goals.

Specific
State what you'll do. Use action words. For example: I want to read more vs I will read three books this month.

Measurable
Make it trackable. Have a target. How much or how many. For example: I want to lose weight vs I want to lose 10 pounds.

Attainable
Make your goal challenging, but reasonable. For example: I want to save $100 every pay period vs I want to save every check.

Realistic
Make your goal challenging, but reasonable. For example: I want to volunteer every evening vs I want to volunteer 1x a week.

Timely
Give yourself time. Set a deadline. For example: I want to find a new job vs I want to have a new job by February 10, 2020.

What are three goals you have for yourself this month?

1. _____

2. _____

3. _____

"Spend today living in your Purpose and make sure you keep track of the results."

Goal 1: _____

Plan to Achieve Goal: _____

_____

_____

_____

Potential Barriers: _____

_____

_____

_____

Solutions to Barriers: _____

_____

_____

Reward: _____

> *"A goal without a plan is only a dream."*
> *– Brian Tracy*

Goal 2: _____

_____

Plan to Achieve Goal: _____

_____

_____

Potential Barriers: _____

_____

_____

_____

Solutions to Barriers: _____

_____

_____

Reward: _____

Goal 3: _____

Plan to Achieve Goal: _____

_____

_____

Potential Barriers: _____

_____

_____

Solutions to Barriers: _____

_____

_____

Reward: _____

Meet The Author

Originally this page served as my bio. After several drafts God wanted more from me. This book was originally crafted in 2015. It started as just a vision, given by God and in every season I failed. As my trials piled up on me, my burdens got heavier, but my walk with God became clearer. The gift we each have is the ability to suffer with God and not without. For so long I chose to suffer in silence. I chose to suffer without God. Every sleepless night, heart ache and battle cry God was on the frontlines waiting for me to surrender.

So, I could use this section to tell you my life story. To help build a narrative and draw you, the reader, closer to me. Instead I will use this section to say just because you cry, does not mean your tears are wasted, just because you're having sleepless nights doesn't mean he has left you. And just because you cannot feel his presence it does not mean he is not there.

God is knocking, so answer — Shanekia Parker Rash

Website: winningseasons.org

www.ingramcontent.com/pod-product-compliance
Lightning Source LLC
LaVergne TN
LVHW010033070426
835509LV00004B/135